PREGRETS

ANSELM BERRIGAN

ISBN: 978-1-7363248-0-6

BSE Books are distributed by
 Small Press Distribution
 1341 Seventh Street
 Berkeley, CA 94710
 orders@spdbooks.org | www.spdbooks.org
 1-800-869-7553

BSE Books can also be purchased at
www.blacksquareeditions.org and www.hyperallergic.com

Contributions to BSE can be made to
 Off the Park Press, Inc.
 976 Kensington Ave.
 Plainfield, NJ 07060
 (Please make checks payable to Off the Park Press, Inc.)

To contact the Press please write:
 Black Square Editions
 1200 Broadway, Suite 3C
 New York, NY 10001

An independent subsidiary of Off the Park Press, Inc.
Member of CLMP.

Publisher: John Yau
Editors: Ronna Lebo and Boni Joi
Design & composition: Shanna Compton

Cover art: *Untitled*, 2012, watercolor and pencil on paper, $22^5/_8$ x $15^1/_2$ inches, The Menil Collection, Houston, promised gift from the Collection of Louisa Stude Sarofim. © Jasper Johns / VAGA at Artists Rights Society (ARS), NY.

Contents

III.

"... *he wanted everything in the picture out of equilibrium, except spontaneously all of it.*"

—Edwin Denby

Pregrets

a century of drawing, endorsed on spine
by the scary amp code for pre-photo
graphic childhood, bystander to a con-
versation (see: religion), micro pigment
ink for waterproof and fade proof lines
sticking out of things, influenced largely
by commercials for plastic toys, forcing
order, Whisp Lou Do (all cutoffs available
via screen in foreground) 0 84511 306
44 8, dark salmon cushion chained to
its couch, interviews hopefully plunged
into process, but (a conjunction) no
loyalty to spatial incidence (produced
as compress), typed arrow, anti-being
in the room, all parentheticals put on
erasure alert, bobble's imitation voice
speaks out from photo dream the other
night, losing lizard count forty-one to
fifteen, fantasy baseball, "your second
wife", liquid net, desire for stuffed goat
to make appearance bound to observer

Pregrets

a side of advance—I makes my way back into
the picture by means of its weakness, atom
of conversation nurses the old projection of
certainty, cold-bloodletted reproduction, elegant
unassumptions studying concrete cracker jobs
for love, insult begets hand shake, I re-enter
through the breach, plenty angrified study
remaking the little explosions that jar us for
further speech, exuberance receives obligatory
promotion, north Irish Carolina yeller
mapmakes it to that reunion—that one over
there—shredded into death by imitation
of skin shedding, & we reconceive the hole
a felt duosity, poking at job despair, hiding
the got money, I'm gonna see all the takeovers
when we get back home, sprocket of violation
velocity girl tag wars, spanster uncles unglued
under thronesters, color products corp verbed
with exceptional sobriety, neighed with extended
exceptional sobrissety, rendered pregrettably
yours with so-called axceptional sobridety, tv
suspended pain-screen-print-fauve-gronk-squawk
requisite ings of postquisite gongs, intermourning
dreams of inversion rhythms playing at pictures
posing in pictures, soft green targets pick me up

Pregrets

after laughter resumes throwing program
95 mph armed growths on trees, blistering
heat feints knock at the local door, peri-
scopically thinking cups decreasing in size
from back of the head extension, tin can
with metal frame on masonite, is the
masonite susceptible to penetra vision
creeping world war, forming itself, into
character, quizzically asks, subtropical
garage door, pulled open by plastic buttons
refuses projections/will not accuse future's
end of living gregariously vicariously or
nefariously off its projection plan &
index funds, obligatory nod to numbers
in form of shaving brush sticking out of
page, I like the vintage floral wallpaper
underneath & expanding away from the
little picture frame, we must have an
activity to play with a feather goes one
pursed mouth or thought, great heron's
delicate investigation, bay at low tide
marauding simultaneity w/ "instrument of
death," preservatives, percentages, growths

Regrets

all you're gonna be doing is serving
mass movement all you're doing in
the service of prior mass movements
all your doings server irreversible alls
moving all your inward logic torn out
to move all your wobbly pieces being
alls moving off decisions to move
bodies all pres are covers to cover
irreversible unknowns all pres are
broken frames humanly stuck behind
some claims to know time by marks
I don't know in my fantasy all fan-
tasies of nonintelligence constantly
jabbed that pelican's an old form flying
by this fish house any pre might be a
plunge breaking down to be anybody's
pieces next to & next to next of & nests
to that ibis sitting there a weird old
form pumping its be next to that arc
of a beak my dig down interruption
interrupted by a cormorant head
popping up all my alls are 2D pres
pitched at arcs to undo as if free

Regrets

boy with brick passes by on way to trick
ending (plummeting in reverse)—puffs
rise, justly impure, breeding kinds off
grids, why would a human regret shit?
I'm not going to run away with the icon
a local wall explained, cautionary Europe
trip, bedding affects between strangers
but the picture plane is being fucked with
by the playground, flat blue bag of floating
snacks just walks itself away, the big bleeding
studio comes down, necrotic red fingers
caught in the casual make, the blonde
is very serious about food, she's a potential
tank injection of stubborn wonder into
the knowy gloom, she's currently eating
the hell out of this rotary phone, she
operates on a post-spliff basis as matter
of course ("You got to give up the flying
saucer baby"), what was I supposed to be
brooding about while shrinking down to
portal-size beyond the self-recognition of
quiet thug punting strollers over the daily
contempt highlighting our scuffed aves?

Regrets

constant hungry undulating surfaces
formed by shit ton of remarks, all invisible
connections as you wrap your livewiring
garmentia about, I'd be peeling back
arbitrarily protective layers all—overuse, twice
use—assaulting some truculent detail at its
haunts—now that's better, the notion
that fish dance preoccupies me, founding
& forgetting to reveal the parasite platform
though given the abundance of self-evidence
for its make perhaps you'll forgive me making
genres out of orificial interstices while refusing
to recognize general definitions et al, but we
mustn't let petulance distract us from the
occasional power of your system of choice
repeating advice, when I walk in & contain
a tremble of average, less than, anti-plottable
—I don't know, sitting down, why we default
to reentry that often, your experience pictures
you from time to time, converting your ice
cloud-addled beginnings into I want desperately
to say bursa sacs, the add on posing as strife
was never necessary, for all the test research

Pregrets vs. Egrets

credo's gumption toasted wishes Christian
Ponder was an emcee instead of a qb, 4th St.
alcools follows the draft down on agreement
to Popeye's dosing frames down Essex saying
saying's pushed off the future spherically burst
organs or what will kick things off, pay to
clean, my needs lying on liftoff at home's
artifice twisted's looking for, my character
set down so as, I get no letter from the
government, predator, I'm not the hit list
just yet wishing lies into strums in my grey
dream fantasies, lift off begrets a so on manic
baroque assertion commute to rooms to brood
over getting it wrong as an agent of relative
time's right to, there's too much light from
above on Clinton St., my sister lived on
Clinton St. for awhile, I walked the almost
mile between old bohome small pov & junior
high for awhile someone like me was always
ready to be fucked with, just to see, my shit
turns every sometimes to what her keeping
live might have been as talk for me, sense
sense, pushing for the visual to make it

Regrets

deads on unleash, four talks fourself
into problems, up 7th walking between
voices describing content, he was 96
he was a doctor, five seconds of glance
at casket, five seconds ago, around the
corner, one week earlier, a painter's son
splashing beer at a storefront, pissed for
what it wouldn't be no more, stations
of the octopus, placed in front of dark
energy, of abstracts, unstuck, how much
of your thinking you think in, description
of interior made adjacent to fight, scrum
calendar closed, now wrong forever, by
the third impaling a lack of finesse
gets exposed, that's a note, scarcity in
lift off, every old face you don't approach
a dealer, sturdy wrecked polis, flipping
off the general makeover, George the
suburban cat jumps three stories down
the airshaft to flee a tenement future, I
tell my daughters stories & lies about
her replacement lately every night

Pregrets

dowery volt cabinet, hurricane funnel, untilled
trop, what now can be affordably ordinary
little pile of bones on shelf in curator's house
but maybe it's the gravity we don't understand
quite happily devoid of any supporting medium
and other stuff inextricably conjoined to the baggage
of your brain, launch fantasycast, ennobled heraldry
in embarcation teased across matching 19th c. tie-dye
dresses, blue & white for phony skylight, with no
plan, free from having to veer, from having to
take off this chicken wire under shirt grafted for
me by the detour himself, spying in the rain on
pocket dial, tongue retaliation shadowed (into
sculpture) by routine impersonation, known
temperance chemistry, a hopeful ventilation duct
blossoming spew, stick a meaning container under
the protrusion glom sweating its surveilled glam
down to skull sulk sucking off the fantasy projection
industry, turtle release at 8pm, the floater comment
to our left, curios dictate/definitions obviate, two
electric clocks sub in to cross eyes in repro, there's
no such chickenwirepie as thing, mass seduction
a warm deet pyre, traded barbs, a struck deal
repeating pavilions of encompassment, John

Pregrets

getting loft and motor oil out of the way
dead ends perfunction—plug-in object
glued to wheel, flatlined into profile
natural orange flavored sparkling heavily
breather in next room gripping multiples
competing hums—fourteen billion years
of cosmic evolution along edge making
spent images today—pigmento micro
taunts sacrificing solo innards action
tumbling into one line gently dividing
a windshield in two—local guardian's
image pops out a fade into plant life
as striation of seated character—kitty
pryde's knee on the assemblagist's
attention—sockets in a box across
the slats—tangerine burro trots by
a tire, leaning—me to means aperturial
stack of apocalyptic tenors shaped up
into ate heart—vinyl sunburn speaking
privately with yellow trunk flanked pink
camp suitcase chair filled with shells

Pregrets

how many bites the glance at the cosmos worth
tonight, palmetto bug with handheld bellows
threatens, on an inward suggestive tip, a take
over of directional collection—correction?—we
get those confused, phrasingly, tin can pocket
watch & chain plate, untitled, sclatchings into
bereavers, bodies unerringly ripped apart &
ponderer, you may or may not build your images
into a likeness of my picture, first take away
the hills, distracted from sleep by hadrons
& their typos, divisions of seconds, grets freely
hatched, dinky asymmetry the cause of so many
chintzy allegories educating your hapless ass
into poorly rendering star charts, by day
a shallow bay, night a phosphor menace
of a surface, flashing hypno-vizio-green
without contradiction as in the dahlias, black
ballast to balance the construction, sharp olive
green, brown & black accents of holothurians
an operating room atmosphere, arms don't bend
like that, composed yellow close red, a and to
with, an abandoned idea for a pic? to count on
the take apart, get back to the spaceship, chickens

Pregrets

minimum wake: fuck the organic exactitude
of the model! Unless, too, Rhyme is made from
oil, fabric, paper, enamel, pencil & synthetic
polymer paint with necktie, fuck it as well!
& fuck gently the sordid sorrow of fractional
& promised gifts, diversion to scroll, the
establishment of incomplete unity would like
its finked deproductions back, for further
scan reduction, & pissed in the photon soup
kick junk, what else can a porous tv rerun
invasion staring sadly out a chapel window do?
wise noncommittal magenta oil stain, in its
epic outdatedness, does not know how to
struggle correctly, does not await its takeaway
can't distinguish between the bungle, the bundle
the bugle, the bagel, in order, to liberate word
& letter, lately folks like evacuate as descriptor
foreign films budding the vehicle shared by
agoraphobia & sonogram-driven desperation
everything looks like a cave painter's horse
tulip snails chowing barnacles, the dignity of
the slab breaks off something stolid, not enuf
shitty function in paradise says the black
moustache drip in lieu of survival as flatness
drip drip drip drip drip drip drip drip drip

Regrets

not reading 'properly'—too slow, too fast
too loud, mind-eye split, too dumb, impatient
too much known to be patient w/ a page's claims
to knowing, too polite, not tired enough, not
high enough, can't see anything, can't retain
process, implode, give in, too much spite
towards hints of judgment, too much desire
for the digressive/explosive diction self-rhetoricized
into passive ideal, too much indulgence of sound
not enough projection, not enough big sloppy
American projection onto prosaic flatlined story
not enough belief in argument, not enough
machinery, not enough soft edge, not enough
shamed temperament on the lackadaisical
interpretation front, too much detachment
from character, not enough faith in allegory
no faith in allegory, metaphor, objectivity
interrogation of the construct while letting
another be made, too much selection, too much
suspension, not enough obliteration, too much
recognition of chaos as shapely, too much patience
for the jam to make its cuts, not enough listening
too much, too . . . too . . . too much listening . . .

Pregrets (beginning with two clauses by Clarice Lispector)

"one doesn't confide everything, for everything
is a hollow void," a hollow void followed by
the permission to be satisfied, I've learned
so little crawling inside what passes as detail
the size you up head to toe & shake don't
work, standing & watching the people pass
no longer admissible, I shouldn't have, any
day then, but inquiries investigations &
interrogations were wasted, wasted on research
& references & ramifications of potential dis-
closure, then I was experiencing yearning by
the mental mantle of a roadside, let's try this
again, here comes an animal sculpture name
of frogina, frogina would like to be less climb-
able in the polluted wonder of everything's
theory, the densely populated local version
of hollow void, impossible to confide in if
easy to miss, for all its infantile overstock
one's empty & secrets & possibly too decent
& probably so kind as to destroy volume
altogether, the narrator, I fear, is fitting
conditions around the typist, the typist, facing
obliteration, & in too close, fears otherwise

Pregrets

put a little box with stuffed bird & toy
pistol in the bobbing footrest filled with
dessicated millipede husks, do dessicated
millipede husks, and humanity, matter?
light socket in pant leg fetishizes the X
out, nodding inside a bitchin' taxonomy
of agreement, head w/ busted can lid sorts
its stuffing: oil (ears) newspaper (nose hair)
fabric (eyebrow scar) wire hanger (lonesome
eyelash conduit) furniture wheel (negative
retina space) zipper (hair line), as for the
rest of the bod: postcard compass paper-
clip and corkscrew on canvas, everything
pitched to the walls is poorly rendered
black box data revealing clues on paper
looks into its soul, sees superpowered
twinsies, cross out "terrible" insert "poorly
rendered" and referent of quiet desperation
(blasted), will be talking to the rays a lot
in the off season, a kingdom of isolation
ampersand it looks like metal's the queen

Egrets

Rodman disputes grisly Kim report ahead
of coif debut blend in space made entirely
from suggestion of nocturnal emissions
shaving down sideswiped consciousness so
as not to post up some pitch of intervention
we're very, very good at fucking up, sorry
again is for the birds, fella teen's response
to role playing pregnancy was change my
unregistered unread number, world con-
struction on the take sets off in multiple
rectilinear conditions trying not to be one
thing, instrument of sentiment, one does
one thing, one withers, bird on one leg
highlights boy dump off-white give off
w/ money life, badgers a complex into
attachment in passing vehicle the things
is always not what you're watching think
the thing is not so ugly as think, Pascal
abandoned by numbers in the dead of
the bathroom light, bends action away
from its endorsements, we underused blue
fingertips but not the tasty thumb, someone's
gotta come construct a construct in the this
for me, gotta cuff the image plane, one only
controls the scarring & scaffolds so much

Pregrets

suggestive tips, cardboard splayed in its own
image adjacent to all that dumped memory
french suites of degrettable expression leaned
on buttons, come here cigarettes & comic
books, defeat the clusters of postapocalyptic
chapter arrangements storming the local
inertiazone & its ageist sun, every red letter
in ACE fucks up the plank depth (bon
voyage metaphysics!), do occasionally choose
the artificiality, for me, of the exclamation—
hibises or hi ibises? registering for the self-
imposed image with azure pump producing
opaque azure bubbles to chase across scans
thirty-three photographs in seven days
charred, beheaded, exploded, or otherwise
fatally injured children scrolled down a screen
I own, the planet out of the way, life inside
structure, fading structure begets its opposite
sky appears, leaky cardboard running off
nameless color, hideous hands kick off a
stroll along a permanent wound's perimeter

Degrets

the skull purses exchanged bitter remarks
&, exasperated, fled across the feels, New
Sauce summons its little family, to model
in intimacy, it's lately blooming homemade
mask, caught stealing fabrics employed cudgel
& stiletto merely grazing, Sigmar pokes you
a sidebar, that hawk laying eggs on an a/c
rallies a cam to live by their side, ornamental
framework falling, broken window glass falling
flaming boogers falling, hypothyroid agency
rising, iron riddled half liters of blood running
free, taser-fed symbology awaiting finesse, think
of the many shits passed this week, suggestions
routinely become physical, to abet & abut the
population explosion, the legs of which remain
asleep, skaters known for their bloopers &
leaving by flying saucer soone enough spending
afternoons working whatever it is out fused labor
& work long ago, for all the goods did them
last zebra screensaver holds serve, invitation
to become pauses, big signature warns you
are not alone, below and to the left a face rolls
around its face, watching you take a break

Pregrets

upsided down self-portrait by elder daughter
sees through the scaffolding of his and his
conceptions, speaking as a haphazard encounter
of a few lines, a few colors, a few shells, a few
insects, a few detours, a few toxins, a few lies
a few fade patterns, one definite assertion, the
accidental order for the lost instinct has to take
the shake of its measure, feed's full of burnt kids
every day-glo cutout, inert, key lime irritant, foxy
beads, the essence of the shit so rich in isolation
elusive even to irrationality, happy sox pictured
in plastic studio setting up the deep steal again
& again on film in the boards, under the little
flash, the little pileated shop worn mask, someone
just walked in & took their time's photograph
I don't wonder about the miniature objects lining
up in me not so secretly, all illusions currently
in the shop, which is all air, for instance we're
writing in sentences, nothing has to be having
matter, want to say a few words about lino
engraving refuse to insure the backup drive
the stand-ins a gang of vicious holograms
in defiance of their own needs and so forth
Matisse was ambivalent about words, words said

II.

Regrets

I told the apparently latent little box I was
slapping myself recursively, long live the down
with, the box frame, the howdy human condition
but I was relaying re to pre to avoid having to
admin it, but I was lying, like now I'm just trying
to remind your yous I can do this, being a thingless
telephat on the hill so as to speak as, give my love
to the air out there, the sets of smacktivated paces
I was ordered to kill a spider yesterday, more
pesticides for me and my roots, I should look up
the origin of out of the blue idiom, but you can
decoratively do it for me, with a sagacious hose
in the alley, an alley priming its pump in another
world, alas, sitting here in cold anonymity, someone
who doesn't dig me, platonically, walks in werewolf
specific shirt rips, that wall is being red flashlights
called upon by irradiated day-glo yellow fold to sit
watching the game on radio, don't you ever draw
on a napkin with my pen again you little winner
in the seventies the adults could raise money
during the day and still hate dinner, now we're
supposed to be complex, never broke, and critically
violent while dissolving the masks of subjectivity
well, *we* are—*you* don't have to care about that shit

Regrets

I have a magic healing fluid in my left hand, a need
to feel cloned by pursuit, prepping for decisions in
a police state, dead artists painting cars in photos
in used books, red with peopled outlines, I failed
the biographer, it was a practiced collector at the
time of print, suppose you're really finished, in yellow
subtitles, you uninspired, untalented fake? bottle
bottoms in permanent face-off, til the rent's too high
again, you're right to laugh, were those ashes once
students, when delirious asking for peas no, no, lay
down, don't bore yourself big arrears, on the come-
backer loop, you don't die sooner because you make
a will, I regret the miniature tracking collapses, the
manipulation of hypothetical drama, all the stupid
locales I never could see, figures on screen in their
pants, running so shamefully fast, I checked the
spaceship, work is progressing well, let's go fuck up
another planet, let's replace & replace & replace
come did you whom with, the ground's a rough slide
into duration, that massive sun folding itself out into
view of our pre-Bellona, all specific threats getting
paid behind their cameras, he's confused, what he
really wants is his plural you to be different from
what you are, your courage to go on burying things

Regrets

not breakding down to a stop in front of paper
whales, purposefully disappeared toys rallying
at airshaft's bottom, oily day stone spasms
raindropping on a stadium seat, crayon & pebble
& ripsnort & fissured ceramics on the windy
surety of Troy, eating prickly pear cactus with
owl eyes in a logical broth under backlit volcanoed
democracy, pink fracking drill bits for the cure
a long slick yellow leather slob ticket w/ blue
spanch across snoopy, forgetting to cover stain
with paper birds, forgetting to spit—ptui!—on
my c.v., my misattenuated bollocks on sale for
free, dude I barely don't know starts following
me, only my phone knows, buffalo lube, little
maroon box filled w/ spills here, turning over,
eaves dropping barrel bombs, lying up, current
continuity notwithspeaking, seeking moderate
opposition guns in the mid-middle just for 'the
record', cardboard pillow pain tube & other
materials, canvas on canvassed, becoming deco-
rative parakeet gouache, arriving late to date with
mercompany, accepting hand sanitizer from
well-dressed bumhaters, failing to cut a small
bird from swiped typing paper, posing wilde
beesties in front of fleeced paint, hanging
brains on speechiness, letting lips fall apart

Regrets

I shouldn't be yelling at these little ones
so often, I shouldn't put them through
yelling how much I despise finding myself
yelling, a cruel Russian doll of stupidity
I call myself stupidity hereinhere and
force a flat feeling into view between this
and you, sorry about that, I lack many life
skills, yet the form's renewal when you sends
back the gap with check to lonesome box
all the way over where, my being from a
colossal nobody there, draws a crowd's
blood from its late figurative style, I don't
know dick, I administer all punishment
get broken down to my constituent parts
cyclically, each one reverts to complex
symbol marinated in non-poignant oils
Tom, Dick & Harry being nasty, oblivious
vaguely reticent embargoes of continuity
if society is truly breaking down, it's not
happening fast enough, for myself, as a
parent, I have to bake pain into the plastic

Regrets

pulled a leaky black eight from my right hip pocket
bought back all my pics & put my foot through them
couldn't tell diff between nit & flake, popped a
wheelie hole in my short term just this past week, or
reasonably like time unit, didn't chuck phone into
east river, silently ripped on the recycled chant prosody
at climate's march, couldn't fansplain downs to K
repeatedly, ever feeling guilty for not learning to drive
confused and forgot about the inner and outer elements
made another fucking list, said writer instead of poet to
the customs agent, wrote out the determining and vital
element in the inner one, which controls the outer form
just as an idea in the mind determines the words we use
& not vice versa, which is fucked up because words
totally determine ideas in the mind, but no painter's
gonna know that, half-spat on all hashtags, dug Botticelli's
abundance without the color, remembered stealing the foot
through pictures unit, but not where I put it, not calling
back all my fucked up friends, simmering, sometimes I go
through real periods of despair, painting the airport mural
freeing association from the start to the finished way to
create my own despicable earth, the barren road of deco-
ration, true purism, preconceiveds, having respected a
certain internal order, telling the ghost hairball story to
my kids, telling the Wystan on the moon story to my kids
making making art be lifelike be my objective, discovering
painting with oil, coloring a dead man, continually drawing
from nature, forgetting to wash these ridiculous clothes again

Degrets (imitation of self)

lucien of doom, colored by occasion, well that's not
especially fair, my big bulbous respirator of a conq-
uest, I dedicate all my evacuated apologies to the
offended if clauses of the western picture plane such
as it secretes allegorical kinship with the practice
of press conference, the tonal torch thus passethed,
text meat back, directors see all the animal stupor
but we observe all the rancor flatness beats off, the
guts to be misshapen, the guts to reek wildly on
the wings of assassination, upgrades suck, among
other local toppings, as little lies go in little lights
hopping off the mad aves, unbanned from life, to
unbutter the same pants wearing day after day, &
day & day & after days & ons & so many happy
acks desperate when up someone who doesn't
know me, speaks through me, but the materials
I was unhandling, the unpan, the unspaced plane
how much unshit you need, going out to the edges
of the unorganism's I would like to indulge all your
vices at once, on second sight this shit's an unad
for thinking, you know, put that this on aslant of
there's my lazy-assed unmenace, awkward channels
& their vaseline coated bodyguards, tacit unity
you owe your unselves many hallucinations

Re to Pre to De

plastic exspectating spreads out as film, to be
being read in & by & for boxes, who gets to play
fatigue & fatigues, every someone getting shot
making openings, who times their delivery ahead
of time, we've got a lot of bad habits ready for
production, who isolates your rage when you
need it as host, chasing light on command
from a stroller, every 'every' inventing a badge
how will you get all cops out of your mind
without deposing your juice, art of the empty
threat, its ongoing practice, raising kids against
custom of mowing down darker bodies, keep
passing on a rigged game, who really wants you
to be persuasive, to have that intangible step
bathing in taxidermied analysis, on sight of death
stirred to distention, disaction, transparent
distortion, little launches for blazing complaints
to comply with, posing as addressee, setting
out wearing spirit-import facepaint of skull-flat
solemnity, traveling in the banter of minor
recognition, squared by guilt, howling in outrage
at misassigned winnings, choosing ticks of violence
to abhor & embrace, ignore & obey, colorize
& fuck, calmly at distances from calmly on fire
walking any blood-drenched rhetorical daze to
schoolishness, a button-pusher's peace, a real private-
like real, reconditioned into weaponized reproach

Pregrets

brain will skip these stations in both directions, black
out blink on the mind, on-the-go transit info kiosks a
hit, you know Planned Service Changes didn't do it
the Degas rehearsal dancers in their slasher flick masks
didn't do it, the El Greco portrait of St. Jerome's hung
too high over the fucking fireplace to do anything, no
grip to lose, happy bestriding a grotesque fish, decom-
posure on mantle, innocent of alienware gaming grunts
open to unremediated flowsure of misperceptions, ding
set for news, there comes unnameable horror, an endless
scroll of possible names to choose, or here goes, rococo
twist of sconce and reflection, Admi, Ado, Annihi, fella
always dressed only in white, white top, white slacks
white egg shell cap, white mutterings, for years nearby
picks up flattened can, halfway across 3rd & 1st's white
ladder walk, chucks it, in the nw corner trash, cult of blue
sky's derangeable mail campaign ass-ready to interject
q-tip's voice following body from room to cave to slide-
walked afterpath, handwriting an only drawn idea
accords with the choke-enticed ocelot at the animation
pit, slant shack swallows shadow snack, all this time
banished, let the ghostly remains go image, hope it's a
sweet cost, let the ghostly remainders scatter, or move
let remains of a ghostly image remain, you better move

Pregrets

I heard nothing but a pneumatic hiss covering
the A's for the chronicle, between pinches of pink
houses & half a life, jersey 14, unsteady among
the retains, investigating the handsomely paid
swaddle state tigers, ready to eat on paper, on
delacoixtic others, analogies on radio checking in
with prudential halos, cardboard spine saggy
baggy's broader concepts of depth & versatility
meant having things sticking out of them, "I have
no reaction to my own texts," sold to sell shifts
from essential to dispensable, told to take a line
for a walk & colour it in, municipal residual waste
rig wet & rolling by, oldly bathed raygun turns the
corner, spins past one defender, o benevolent ones
enfold me lightly, now I see I've had concentric
wrong all these times, a certain nausea sets in on
our outer rim, is it emerald, lime, sour apple
chlorophyll, or ochre plains circa Red Cloud's wars
in white man's books, snack request attacks the
sequence, neon evergreen pizza sign behind low-
hanging avenue leaf scatter, brightlingsick green
abandoned tote on dark green granulated rubber
ground spiked with gated play, acidic toddler hands
ass poem for a wipe, transparent puke orange bud
bus ads itself along, cased color no-bothing line

Degrets

Fools do as doom requests, fungoid pulp, forgive
our backs, forgive the figurines standing on their
heads in front of the citadel, its reflection more
finely detailed than fact, daddy's wipey pincers
in the pre-selection pool as attorneys prepare to
sue each other's sides, you wouldn't like pumpkin
orange when it's sad, generic x-sections of massly
proto-received instructions are our civic duty of a
speciality, boppers inside lineup, elegant smears
upended within noun-verb rhythms, you post the
same shit in different electroid space-likenesses,
why no little electric shocks? why are we such
suckers for repetition? why the goal of playing
home repairs eternally? why so few eye-bag tattoos
says self to dinky self, I feel sorry for the future first
floors, I guess & guess & get happily abandonable
vis-à-vis e-town meetings, would I be a big blur, sub-
mittable to roaches' theater, we don't actually need
congress anymore, cities of water deadlocked, anointed
to consider scenarios, & I seriously fucked over all
the hinge language, petadogically speaking, under
relatively stable & not directly oppressive governerds
corrected it, whatever it is, boils down to sifting
through your various shits, ostensibly, maniacally
indubitably & (insert prefix)bolically speakering

Regrets

experience's hot lime american diaper, coaxing its
megadeal hoax out of retirement charges, pulls hook
from back & names them rendition, maybe I've made
enough of an impression, when it comes down on it
when it comes on it, when it itself soothes solitude
into the pen, bendy design busts little holes in arbitrary
guts, tampering charges filed against jets, my brother
loaned a magic hand to a bystander, circles cleaned out
eating communities leaky-heart style, the most beauteous
soft wear ever diluted, life flashes plastic ass across screen
I can't beat June at hungry hungry hippo, I can't untie
with Sylvie at zingo, dudes dudifying misdirect pressure
but that's always been that, here, have this pic of a bag
filled with bad blood, it's very bright said nurse Boris
& ever since my thought balloon's been filled with wings
drooling to a shatterpoint, what you figure death adds to
you after it finishes erasing, I can almost listen for how
my dads smelled funny, you ever carry your dad's pee
in a jar, little technician of the sacred, butter and
whatever's left in the fridge on bread, hand me the phone
dial this number, get the book out of your pants, Doug
taped a Doug Strange card to the wall we gave him
his body, gone so quickly, deep into the humor well
they're so fucking funny, funnier than all that invisible
money, when I was nine I heard the otherwise mute
summer bum once say he was surprised they don't
drop bombs and grenades on this place every day

Pregrets

just leave a little unfinished feeling on the edge
there somewhere, disrespect your given indentation
you know, sounding like some idea of talking, fuck
that, with the angular nearness of objecthood, its dis-
equilibrium & rational miscomposition & congrats
you're a dissolute piece of seriousness undergoing
routine axis inversion, & presenting Janeway, on top
of existing offers, we could always gradually reintroduce
the DNA at a later date, elite relievers on the reverse
side, June drew a Twombly, two hundred comments
to go please, he should be rappelling or sleeping on
the sidewalk every day, the copy dosed with gravitas
prepositions for sale, naked taste subject fondles
mechanical buy, mows-down-most-of-the-league don't
wanna sit around the pen watching spankings every
night, big hot pastrami confidant stewed so much it
freaked out rivers, exhausting previewed space, any
minor mix-up might spiral sneeze into piss streams
for some reason I'm always in a good mood, mentally
you ever see weekend at bernies 2, there's already a
dead guy, Spider, Baboon, Bocci, & Pockets, devolving
from scorpions to brothers, edge auto rental bumps
made a little move, didn't have my footing, trying to
sort out the jester market, the domino market, the
classical problem of underexposure to old commercials

Degrets

live updating: the spins, pretty sure the Bears
coveted me, but their needs precluded picking
me, there were safeties available, & their safeties
were junk last year, twine on unstretched canvas
tarp on wood support, then I come to wondering
what a manner precisely is, body exercising stages
of control, distortions of accompaniment, mouth
fighting through evol-flop compression to leap
and leak, but who the fuck am I watching so as
to be talking, who, as the voiceover, doubly
disembodied, puts it, did this to us, oil on rubber
tire and packing crate panel, plates 164–165
because you hid in the walls making work we came
to Cleveland, ink notch resembles consequence
my liver cavity would like to interject, to be winter
twisting the gripes of cripes-crepes hippo groping
between e-chairs, the living room needs a bog to
tie all the practiced refuse together, fear agent
jelly brains evolving from utopian to scavenger
yet we elude proof, the inner crackpot and the
inner bureaucrat are not one, divinity an affect
of habit, is it funny shaped out live like a head
is it shapes assembling itself into origins, or what
passes as recreation, to pitch beats as a plot, now
you got a slow explosion replacing your head, no
one has to fold up a care, days hanging off sticks

Pregrets

Got the imprecise gaze breaking down again, other
times I paint it then I see it, plus the written owl
typos, in time, like I'm not supposed to be here,
doing my this this way, but I am, but so what, &
that's some uncanny two-faced scar-art business
puny somethings, tell me a story so I can fake
sleep a little better, Panthers getting toasted, kneel
unseen on shade dark sunk head turned back un-
changed, back sudden gone sudden, hears pipes in
these legs, legs hear swipes in these pills, progress
busts our irradiated chops post-school, too many
costumes of information, inflotation? infoefoam-
ation?, pumpkins freak me out, in this abstract way
cause nothing concrete freaks me out, exactly, some
folks are turned on & out by exactly, which is a form
of pumpkin you suppose, edge can't, flesh of blind
spot, crow jane systems, nice mild flame reflection
hey baby, the world hates us, crosses enunciate with
emphasis, there's a lot of hits by car on screen tonight
lots of fights to wade into the popcorn with tonight
investigation of incidence, white letters blue screen
mission to mars still ahead, I was broody like a splat
now I'm saying its all ok, I wrote about it at length
after looking at it from a distance, I have to blow
I have to blow now, for a thousand smears, that's
the pathmark, tomorrow knows land's end, eh curly?

Degrets

projection of illegal advertising, zero curvature with oily
exuberance, tiger collar vibration's zoned off leap from
plane to aged plane, the arms are corked, shushed shucks
selling aws & awls in the daze of 20 & 14, wallpaper
menaces pansy, tank division separates beluga bods
at tails, loo goo for goo radio plugs into cardboard
money, action after action after an action imitation in
an action confit bleeding hot pink across frames of sky-
screen, all your chipped teeth look alike, blue leather
hexagonals socialized into "ball" roll up, daddy I'm
hungry pulls arm: you make your kid into an object
to push around between sounds? secreted by muted
rainbow ground pulsing blood, Leger's worker drowned
in a cubist grill, squares, ark leaves, streams of Sunday
piss review the flaking stats of a ramrod dignity, a bearded
curfew with unidentified debris, trailing a moving hole
no, following a singularity, big la & little la in cadmium
rack specifics, splattery affects jonesing for a buggier
emphasis, &, speaking of Guernica's plot reserve
combine-kluh pleasures its axis, where the teeth bend
out at their tops, combing back the slick with a jawbone
watching the watch be watched by remote, matter-eater
lad's death distant & unseeable, streaks of digested matter
shaping cardboard's invitation to sit, lie, drunk image magnet's
resonance taking the chorus out of the kids & turning feral

Degrets

splatter's a Picasso at hitting into double plays
an angry sub-centimeter, lesion sound dictates
a letter, limited time offer insta-cocoons into
bloom luxuries, sporty in parents, first came
the archive, then this next one I wrote tomorrow
sling-enabled, on a to-scale map of our local
galaxy cluster, but the drone's orbit misdelivered
its astral package, sorrow's bleed-space queered
the nudge, the unopened toy sewing machine
went out for surgery, brief company colored in
how to feel, the regular season cuddled in
detached corners, the blurb borrowed a fin
the dunghill bummed a mouth breather, the
multiple pantsed the tranquilizer, the I-left-my-
shell-collection-scattered-by-prescription-to-
rearrange-purple-plastic-bowls-of-birthwater-for-
dolls wintered on, fruit flies landing in rashy
spines, unavailable's gonna have to leave a
message, all items loaded, skeletons snoozed on
mantle, little blue ribbed fuzz mammoth enters
the about part of the combine, eats it, sharing
the shuffle, not the potty, unassailable's gonna
hasten to leave a menace, all refusals in box
in bed, in the screen capture inflected by read

Pregrets

your line drawing is the purest & most direct
translation of my emotion, when I can't see it
can't see the cheap lapdog freedom of the slight
drainy blue coming through Tompkins' trees
(those anti-curfew elms!), mutant delusions
a less rigorous medium than pure line, stretch
(sag), stretch (bag), kick (repeat), hey look, a
trashcan on wheels, working for the city, a view
suffused with anxious frigid white, flicked angels
heavy metal on a cruise, the puckered pronoun's
dressed sky, marble lust compulsion simmering:
to be nostalgic for fear-tremulous fast walking
all the little between spaces, (squirrel drops by
offers assistance, turns down request to help
pregret), words made into oil, flesh, water lilies
ducked out odalisque backs biting elongated
suspense panel, time to unpack ass from bench
the lamppost continues sticking itself together
for a sub-molecular glance, all greedy smokes
making hands conduct air, exasperated text
brings missed boat, the commute betrays the
worker again, zebra-striped hearse in 2-D
leather jacket, on scaffolding premises, big
decorative anti-work, white paint maply shaped
onto green van waving itself along, cheating

Egrets

wind, beast or sea, nocturnal cries, buoyant friends
daily lurk apart, half hummingbird, half eagle, at
dawn smiling I turn out the light, minutely stereo-
scopic, mushroom, a root claw, mosses, underwood
arboreal shadows, moon-cast, near the horizon yel-
lowish, they're so unreal, everyone kind, sunny field
gloomy forest edge, I know them near, feebly I
drowse, buys a ticket to see what's true, prowl car
walk past, at my corner, hurry to ballet, its invention
overflows like a rifled trunk, Jacob from school in
the bus home—that like enraged had roared past me
miracle consciousness I'm with, both have nodded
my way, up the street, who trusts it, but its contagious
tonight the two stray cats here wail, a shack in the woods
the turned switch, coolly on earth as in thought's
joy, obscure voids that my heart munches, sleep against
the push of a cat, felt by homes, felt better by farts, Man-
hattan night, inbound, outbound, she heavy every
which way, groans, storm-dark or moon fog instable
near my shoe, sparkles dark granite, scraps of Park
speech, blown scraps of paper, vulture stranger aswoop
the sky, what's in a name—it regathers, a heart's force
he was going mad, on New York, where we rest unknown
lets them honk, soberly waves them on, savage fighter
playful at night, snow's hash, siren, rain, hurricane, sweet
Europe, you're so comfortable, real disaster is so near us

after Edwin Denby

III.

Degrets

helicopters break the sky into rooms, sonic interiors
short on implacable angles, report myself to graphite
food tasting lines walls, in red stencils, the raft shaft
cousin container, not divided by radar reflector, I
should hurl my glasses from this ferry, but I really
just really can't see shit without them, eek serve
claw nebula bats pillars of creation into panonymity
for Eddie's birthday we took the life vest out from
under his seat, somebody should iron this, dare me
while you're periodic tables in neon, no gore screen-
time for handwriting, which, a la Bigfoot, freaks the
seen, that conservation intern cleaning your head
remains unpaid, someone says disembowel the vessel
every time I start a letter, portal appears to bobbing
skyscraper, silver guy in jeans & olive tie asks immobile
tourist if he's a cop, sets up silver guy shop at bleecker's
mulberry 6 stop, room with interior chat, room licks
room where guitar folds into room with no privacy
imagined me, starry (white) bunting (night blue), held
I hear the old wobbling floor for sale, crane hangs crate
in front of box of sky, I drop like a cat from monkey
bars June says, a severe inability to make contact lets
wave remains empty our bodies, it swings by, loading
standard viewballs, slurred or eviscerated by light
human legs mutating into drumsticks, o lantern
holding up a hackstop, what do you illuminate

Degrets

image production sells us our meltdowns, we con
ourselves into participation, coming on an of at ages
laughter is very very good to the coeval populace
disfigured via comparison with flow, I don't know
numerously, flattened impact players mounting real
madness & ending anti-heroically, even sanity ain't
sane today, disinvited to play Dragon City please
snipers gotta stop ripping off pigeons, first vision's
the vulgar one, sadness tones given by the dark
dominant, a self-portrait all ash-colored, true para-
sites of the object, glad I figured out how to be kinder
to my brother, outside of any unfortunate art please
accept all my regards, zapf explains, your rethought
got rethoughted, or verily skate-ragged & rebesotted
neutrality in shadows, misuse of shadows, when you
put camouflage on I can't see the bummer's rehab
eternal, if to be is the object of resurgence merged
with insurgence, we'll be a nice menu memory
druggy in huggies, replacement level topless vatican
protester who stole jesus free, I used my transfer
drawing to hop on unlimited lead heads from behind
the practiced shadow in a form of public, shape
contains form & moves for listeners listening to
how you say you see walking get held on the aves
the sides the gaps the co-flats the blocks, the peri-
winkle tune symbols gliding down through the locks

Regrets

le leaping newboyish swirl blunted cretinism subs in
scrabble ballast muscle, to be a what costume clocked
on, if you don't shroom slide think anyone's looking
lifted from upstairs aptitude why engage eagle oil
peanut paper on a decision-making level, metal
photograph, fabric, wood canvas buttons, the fantasy
they eventually will, stool screams for a sack, be on
my stride, canyon adapts, special teams pan, eye drop
an elephant on your head module from a stone's
back, no sweat without fruit fly, thrills of soft anxiety
fused ankle, scissors in hand, only his torso was lost
all policy riders in indigo panic punt blockers jump-
ing to touch suckers as rarities, shaky dots denying
entry, resurrection's revenge in cutout light, bobbing
resurgent cowbobs, leg whips in mole space sauce
sleeping at intersections out of the question's abs-
olution, a pain in my lean's asses, driftwood nanobots
& their fake accents head butt on the swing, spider-
style, tawdry shimmies w/ safety features, jarred giant
centipede down twenty at the half, & then I'm joust
like ads against myself half-fast, but the cat waved from
what once was a planet, & the cat waved sliding across
Saturn's rings, & the cat winked out of Jupiter's eye

Pregrets

milking clock with the turd herds enforcing
sentiment from every knowy slant of stage
gold painted A in sky balloon coming paperless
onto post, where else but in fiction can a design
fight with its support & win, I'm officially blood-
letting brotherfucker's spatialized interior flow
across its externalized comport, down with the
related splitting, immediacy's pelicans granted
permission, the detour feeling very solid in the
communal uncoherence, go home juice, no chance
tracking, that thing sticking logo pump lighting
out of your person plane, claiming hug simulations
but only on adult surfaces, rupture a certain settle-
ment in the soul grease, nonstop service from JFK
ain't never gonna write a fucking novel, I stretch
a cardboard barricade across an imaginary table
& refuse a plagiarized request to recuse myself
the open invitation to have anything laminated
was a come on I couldn't bear, a bylaws infraction
bears couldn't bear, tongue winch, thudding oil
on paper, demo zone lot wall says Geno moved
to 11th Street through a diamond view, a blue
baby drips red outline, eye candy for survivors

Degrets

poor Soutine, forehead pouring out from paper
tear of a leg, bred to beastlieve difactual gravitation
the antelope's irreal got-me pose firing on the rum
anything frames anything, the hole with a hole in
its make-out session with a clown blue (gutter) &
gold (roachlight) he looked like 65 when he died
he was a friend of mine, haves or rip, don't know
much about Titan usage, everything's she's a trip
better when, this little shit, you're crying the light
cut through it's own flashback, a shotslung form
armadilliac cliff hanger for your shawl of shellings
front of units conceiving baselines to around's left
offense to run through love, not's no-rap ging-glugged
style: root over rock, old 7 scraggily enough to ignore
doing this in broad something, anything and the ing
of ings mock-strangling via scarf toddled she bids
on launches, on piecioles, death's tourney snapshots
check in with the air's current concierge, death is at
the scorer's table, death handles the small forward
position, the satisfaction survey check-in, I keep
trying to quit underwriting a splicer's crabby pincers
and the cat fire on yr insides measures you when you
speak to think, chilled high villainy in jars on silk

Regrets

roaming charges writing this tomorrow on the drop
off way into nowness, little boy on wall releases shape
yellow painted bird grasps buckle light onto plane
building angles hit up bushy mountains for geo-
metric incursion trips, got to dissolve our opposites
this chair in the corner says call me something else
& don't settle on it, it's messed up to hear, to listen
to the chair, I grew down on a dirty St. block version
a precedent paved the ways for your own approach
I hated those dealers on the corner & hate was a word
I wouldn't use, & some of them were cool with the
fragment that is advice goes hot & cold, your way I like
your way I gauge, your current droopy angelic high
naive composition, I'm big, I use that, and lonely
dance with me, look at those lights, see the other you
seeing me as point of amusement, high but leveled
now a helicopter just staggered by, sometimes I can't
distinguish flat from straight, this also the achievement
talk of the clown face prevents us from recognizing
toast toasted by painter painting a painting, lazy heron
blues pull on the picture occupation's target, "hold
the joint of your thumb close to your eye, it could just
as well be a thigh," heard in imagined voice pinned
near grid baffler, the grin more shark than idol

Degrets

sand winged foot box in canary recall may be
entitled to atoning sacrifice, wood newel cap
blackmailed facetiously by quanta, miscast
recast as stand in, tacky jetty, goodbye into, &
metal wing shit on all over again's chalky out-
lined pliability of chance peeled off the nudist
payphone museums where Titan dreams are
launched, minus the bewildering flatness, on
expensive slum corners, in post-realist brack-
etologies, with help me be beestly pure, children
do the dirty lifestyle migration work, every aud-
ience forgets to relearn speech, on sides, peoples
dig diaper posts, upside filling the boxscore
then I make a hatchet from the iron in my orgs
fashion a nest out of falling glass in what's left
of Astor Place, my pet-balloon canyon state for
the failure of civilization to ever see anything
but itself coming on oil, paper, printed paper
printed reproduction, wood, glass jar on metal
chain, & fabric on canvas equals Talisman
staring into the play out as ump & pear, shoe-
rail & fillet, at special angles butted with coped
end, constellations get happy gliding down
Hosmer's brows to browse the leaving field

Pregrets

tern nesting area near the cannons of Comfort Road
a cross-tabulational analysis, from the just outside part
one time, and for to of with on in everybody, it sounds
like I can't describe it, I'd like to thank life on Mars, run
turn offs resubmit, they'll never have enough predictive
morphic cathedral in falllight, the sleight of death's hand
names have to fail your pain, nudge the mini-geometrics
begging for micro-appellation, (they're not), they would
love to see you at their sister bars, I suspect, my head
freezer services, leaf dust invasion foreshortened by xeno
our client's only regret is not finding us sooner, preferred
wolf in Bryn Mawr, lonely no stopping for repairs sign
the chicken a couch, naming the great dane after a were-
door, servicing all makes and models, the duck is a chair
is a boot, the line never really straight, if there's a back
sorry baby, babe, child, girl, daughter, Sylvie, S, eldest
fractured monkeybar wrist, the hot take pain that arghs
nerdy reflection, death by antlers, fuck the lean into grey-
grey, attracted to folded outlines of scrag bills, severed
head adjusts to its new content, in New York we take
great pains, to spread death out, pat death down, echo
future muggings, the star in fact a rock, insistence is futile

Degrets

tiger uneven texts dark age at night, not just shining
some shiny elephant dung, I see Portugal I see
Spain I see purple's underbrain, costume desig-
nated to implode, calling its pop-up antipathy
fauna, things that could have, mauvely, cyanly
pucely, heliotropically eviscerating likeness, the cat
of yesteryear uses chartreuse power ring to will
a sun-sized packet of tender vittles into slowly
turning to pour upon the big blue marble, your
work with the whole room being part of it, oil
on feathers on wing bone goth broth, "a diversion,"
goes immutable emotively immobile elven face, do
you know hard it is to catch a monkey, hello dear
I am writing this, "ducks defeat predators," with due
respect, & heartily of tears, since we have not known
or met ourselves previously, dosed toast followed you
looking for some juice on the wing, you really think
& fuck it?, they thought things looked like that
since now its mc commons for workaholics to be
placemats anywhere in a room, it's muy impossible
for placemats to understand that poems on the floor &
the absence of a pedestal were inventions, you (& your
no-history's less than seriously fucked) invented them

Pregrets

touch anywhere to resume, dilacerations outside
like lenses waiting to be focused by the giant squid
everything's better when you're crying, systematic
& humane, I need a spliffed roof of a head over
my causeway, strata collar plays giant slacky thwarts
try mouth, sweet dawn skate glut cheese fanks
"rounding third or so we heard", rosy awaits dry
blue, choky bubbled ropy, the fuzzy hummer and
me dig rhyme's concave ditch into yeoville, reach
fingering slide, mid-replacement, play free now
outchilling by itself, corner trax muted as thingless
box fighting purse, excoriate the with usage, scare
kids into happy & piss off the alienated tender
into further fader toggle, dads trim grunts, waverly
dewy fluffs, encrusts bursts in the chaos intakes
unlike likes dandelion time out, I shook so hard
I scared my kid into seeing a glimpse of me as
content, felt hedged preferment, pastel grids curve
dread, sipping clunky nursed version of here
slipping off slicklight's greaselight edges, all the
local loving knows to ignore you writing up against
a leisurely wall, what's up spiraled noggin face

Regrets

touching tingles stomach, I wanna be a dolphin
that has a dress on, you be the monster, nag a ram
tonsils threatens to whap me two thousand times
with little guy brohennas in victor, elaborate scooter
diplomacy, she sentences tattooed constraint luck onto
brokenness in victors, breakfast slaughtered landscapes
my name not Emily, annihilation times verge of
tears, solar system's apparent velocity cubed cars
fucking all bods, plural chunks of ice matter clapped
onto driven incapabilities, all you fronds with defensive
affinity-optional features, shown on shelter, relative
color relates baton to bacon, swings it in fingers, gazes
blankly, whiles, talks, oils shape, takes it off again
puts it bach, runs fingers around the inside, feels it
off country-like into finalise, plays with nightcap
empty bile ductlings, one sweeps, wrecks of the prior
what had us, mobbing for discommitment inside
the how do we live as zones, inside z, you want my
high res shadow frolic capture, deep centricle give
the storefront slats a bubble, insta-elf storaging, I
hoped each organ to fall out, work livening paradise
slurps, no good texts to godself, back lot booster
that dumpling the elder shit too shorts the clause

Degrets

weirding spotlit apertures, cormorant neck in hell's
gate grey, oathkeepers patrol the fringe, making images
of controlled insanity, a closed cube unborn to non-
interior, the blues come forward, white a deathly
institution, cross concept punishing armature, inert
reflectivity is a sign the interior ruptured pineapples
are cloning, coming, outwards seep, recesses shooting
up ink is what the de fantasizez over, the spaceship
snapshot of the former planet lay plainly on my
desktop, green-like blue-like oil-like red, cylinders
float stuck-like, to what techno was when, no window
blues assault an illusion of light into the body hole
fold me, creature in male skin lurks between stranger
& corner, I test the lock politely, this other person
recedes into rent, sometimes I'm cool with the colors
being flat, mantle thumps behind my spine, wash
tannins off mugged conscience, should I read this
shit in progress to the wifi stranger to my left, phone
dead you can't find me, who can't quite understandably
the understanding platform eraseth, wear the whether
suits, I'm a skin that bears slovenly dress to uphold
a counterpro invisibly, there were hole histories in
every body that spoke, directly or half, near & to me
the ledge commands a conclusionary charcoal magenta
smog the others stammers a gentle subsidy to go

Degrets

all the K's rise as yellow squares, now that trivia's
run its course, livesofts soil through the entrails of
post-knowledge, time feels up a slight, I just helped
the folks to my right cheat at general knowledge
no grexit, hell is other corporations, on the Budapest
Airport chainmail list, white terrorism cuts the oxygen
midrange, active, long, grazing in the graveyard rode
an elephant in the zoo on your head, then I rode an
elephant on your eyes, previously suspended, ideas've
no idea how hard it is to attempt twenty short poems
in a glaze, I hear them literally running unconscious
interference, & dude walks in to take everyone out
again, giftwrapping chips around my heart in honor
of alone time, human summons light, to prove, and
be proven, it's not so hard to give up everything, it's a
matter of exchanging voices, postcorpse started follo-
wing you, it's very hard to retrain your listening, I've
got this cost for about, I keep it permanently loose
somewhere around way over there I'm a covered base
levitating carry-ons into sub-extinction to achieve a
feature, lean flake jimmies a lake where I gather
roofs raise eyes, today Picasso, hidden in a casque
w/ crested plane, freaked me out, pointed panik chins
way to transfoliation, tinge of wobble, messlessness

Degrets

bombing for a third space, between enemies, brushing
permission, forge & paper plate on $2500 painted news-
print, between astro and shag green preveals tractor
phones beamy feels, so they all, select to say, the plastic
life terribly dangerous according to the in-between, cast
pressed, protruded into j-v terror, perpetually ambiguous
pharmacy therapy played out as soulful politics, plus dog
fucks dog, enter Q-train light, Chegra white flat out
forward in so-called time's turquoise armies of letters
blod s olve, do not lean on mechanical twins, job place-
mentat assistance available, every dude's a suspicious pa-
ckage, objectively speakingly, she's dead wrong, but she
wields her prismence on screen with stubbornity, unfo-
lding the priority tsunami tseat, yellow subway floor thing
between fruit & plastic fractaling, a shimmer no matter
on or if or as or in gems surrounded by tortoise shells
faked or sealed, subgressively pregretting the artifice of
chemistry, pant leg, necktie, mattress pad fragment, in
its deposition to Nature, matchbook cover & found
wood sigh on canvas, aquamarine urban ears in pseudo
recovery of attention shift, cosmetic ground, pursuant
of misregistration to the last, J saw milk paintings in
daglit kickback & asked if she could touch the comfy
spots again, hyperchromatic treat day canceled forever

Pregrets

caution tapes participants yap commotion tells
us to blow patience into strangers edge rental
said be fine that broken body had a being in a
humor consortium lean your body in without
leaving the line hold things up make them pay
random potable twenties in eighties sampling
shoebill dreaming of digging lungfish up & into
greater koodoo today pre-combine background
measure if you're not a stuffed turn around the
diorama following you flashfloods eternity confro-
ntation with gemsbok sunflower helmet leans
into ribcage near elephant model oldling ob-
serving through glass eyes do they really never
see me really never really with sand on your
tushy and pantry pests a nice enough piece
of sense trade-in required the humongous
tentacle erupting into golf tourney asks what
vulgarity means it's one of the forms of life a
book in reverse farewell replies conquerer in
red projection the beach an edge of ground
for matter factual monstrosity approval ceases
to be linear soon as it makes appearances word's
root upending your littlest parts for starters

Pregrets

deanimate squeaks harmonize hula hoops evolving
squabble, I'm constantly almost smacking perma-fear
into, we almost knew each other's variegation, fire's
on screen, the tender's bag's blowing pipey wind
iconoclastic in the submergent future, another one
was the phial, any snakes nearby, they even moved
like you, puice in the ghosthouse, retinal anecdotes
their backs, skywritten, are turned to you, next to
being ridden dimensionally, you're the eohippus
the D is the jockey, since my groom loon's doomed
on the glass, he's flat, ready to be inverted into pictures
the filth-ridden Titan phone booth a few feet north
to the right lives in fear of painterly execution, efficient
Boozer adjusts to role on bench, following pseudo-
pseudonym, a grasshopper swimming with grasshoppers
old dirty classic of the period, imaginary dingleberries
stank-optional, I need these things out now – I might
be dead later, I'm not expecting fragment bump, fall
away bump, pile on & still exude bump aura, reverse
the outer corners until specific arrival mandates itself
into existence, hi Satan, your schemes lack gmos & bpas
& rbis, & contested amphibian blunt imitations, yays
the re-ape for the Divine Mystery of the Universe is an
open secret, as I just got told by a firm, a rapid, a very
agreeable transparent, no, flesh-colored premise

Degrets

drawn frogs appear to serve the exoskeletal goddess
in full mollusk shrug, shelves built for dated wreck
registers, cranial outbursts finely detailed, opening
at the outline of a spotlit ribcage, lists of thefts enter
micro-entry zones, respectability a possessive monster
needleteeth palms, languorous working in a front of
poured-in window light, off-white airshaft blue pushing
forward into the flatness of a room masquerading as
two, wears out a corner, somnambulist soap preformance
trickles along, black & white docufilm footage of
fam's thing-strewn space makes way into numbered
views, anyone may anonymously enter the screen
version of your interior & very few will, column of
skulls stands up a bulb socket, speed hump ahead
15 mph, minnows twig-hopping, playing pick up styx
in the hydroponic vape church fuming newness outs
of touch, & truth kicks back at a fool's conception of
neutrality, thump thump kids need to stop falling
out the bed, ghost marooned on sock induces mock
shriek from the subaquatic generation I raise on stay
or no cookie, network name: true, like & hurt go
hand in hand, the zebraic cosmologic selfie rides with
a drone stick, acktility expenses, tick trick carriers
careening into snake shapes, sonar belts aura mouthing
activate instead of turn on, to radicalize a golden
tongue, dig the corpse & call it rotary possiblimity, we
just can't help wiping the weird out of intelligence

Pregrets

duly afflicted by changeling light, I beg you command-
eer buttons, rubber wheel with electric fans where we
chase the headley, that's what I'm paying tire tread
on wood with chain and flashlight for, internal server
errors & bummers unite, do what you want, stretcher
dropped wound to run, brain with bear hanging out
back of its head, minus manic to be emphasis, how do
I even who like to myself's a sound's question, on the
subtitled proto-make laying some first eggs for drawing
spies like dust, let the electrical junction box coming
come, did bibi ever finish his speech to the hack & tool
brigade, open tanking the melting across vortexical
slushlight, incendiary antic blends a conservative gots
to wield as yield costume playing with bends, & like
rhythmically that, articled orgiastic instacore hemorrhaging
on cue, the clunk bus, nah I'm just sitting over there
mad at its not drunk, permissions request dolefully
replaced by crab-grabbing octopi, compass & passbook
sharing projected fecal explosions accredited to event's
horizon portrait, gives the deadpan evil eye to a zone
out posing as at work, considering multiple offers
bleachable moments & bleachable shields, fabricked
adult-ass plumb bob, turn a blind grid fragment of yellow
rubber life raft, hey dig dog, open panting, dumpling go

Pregrets

fleshy Rubens got crazy about the crazy duelist's
bodywork, solidity and color messing with us
again, definite order's customary crisis kissing
any disembodied ass it can find, we took the real
from the representation & gave it rent-free floorless
housing in the horsehead nebula, otherwise I'm on
4th street near B & another Anselm's around the
corner on B near 4th, fainthearted ska repentance
blaring through idities, vanishing your egg & glue
your right to gloom so entirely yours in entirety
fondling surfaces again little chalkboard, little
screen, little wing pattern evolving into surf sobs
through alien speakers, plague flags party in kiddie
colors, cats, copying, my ten favorite books suck
clambers up to clamor's stock b'eau de lariat, da
nation retweeted behind the fear of color cover's
a cat catching scents to keep clear of sense, Jo-
hnny Air Mart evergreen awning across ave A
self-compartments in bunny balloon reflection
on the chaseway ornament lobby trail, iv contrast
charcures the abdomen for fleeting preservation
the abstract poet runs where in cognito again? my
time's draino down the crosshatch, I'm a patient toy

Regrets

goodutopian liked your specter chained photo to we
disagree about how! to organize the bodega society
light exchanged blam for kooky, & me without my
more denim head, I stole a shitty yesterday, couple
wants my table but they will wait forever in my gulpture
in terrified tears I got on the bus & never saw dad
again, but in a perspective of feeling, emphasis declined
zebraic cosmologic steals negative bases, when I run
for anti-president no one will get e-mail barrages asking
for chip-ins, is that a bleeding tautology, a genre of
children's freedom pleasing art: a selection, I began
with a diminished profile, but from what no one need
ask an asker asks, on the coming battleworld, all micro-
histories in limited run, what shit I sent myself recently
for to compose around this received spread of pain, I
don't dig-think a need, the last thing I get to say, never
clear what enough is, when the mice died I killed the
painting parent survey deadline, student hare, so, Man-
hattan Luck, too many persons to occupy a step from
now the little box, once a booth, calling for transient
gasp of occupation, what about always looked so alive
I felt really sorry for that poor dusty dirty filthy goat
by the sixth or seventh drink Billy stopped talking base-
ball, if all those fingers were disembodied now, we have
to be realistically oppohectic, I spent more money on
shampoo to get the goat clean than I did buying it

Regrets

too tired to be the monster, every thing's the wrong
blind spot warning mistaking the comforts of legit-
imacy for words, naked lovers of wisdom hoists a
three, amazingly few movement motives used, con-
fession use, vanity divinity caress, a helmet-to-helmet
blow, which involved no helmets touching, red pur-
gatorial tire swing making angles over leaves from
the spins, the leaves gently raise ground as names
of convenience fail to reappear, names vanish into
sound, a walled-up camera disappears into condo-land
mildly fascist brunch snuggles with livers, complicity
traitor favorited live, fleetingly, no time for poems
with all this e-sociology poised to bite in disparate
need of absolute paragons, dressed on the cheap
warmth installed, hyperreflective office bunny goes
glass, pen explosion hair, gets a touch of the old iron
filing, receding into a shammy cottage, playing at
parquet reserve, stick a flat bug fiat onto prosody
plane, call it sub-local divinity for lack of a common
splaffect to disabuse of urgent withdrawal, we are in
view through diamond cut into torn down theater site
brought to the shop to enliven assigned elegies, all
potential seeing things run themselves, like, away

IV.

Degrets

how much time wasted waiting to be loved
unable to identify any love coming, there's
the end, it can't even pretend to stop, words
collapse into your movement, a gym of gestures
you pay to sweat within, in honor of something
like extension, lines enter our ears, lines swim
before our faces, we enable brutality against
our wishes, which are barely known to us
& that's a lie, we're too many to know, &
why isn't a flower a star, if nothing else is
available, you can have your wise translations
you have them already, your whole sense of truth
is fed laterally, pity the applied ending, it's only
a desperate face commanding us to begin again
if the hook wasn't sound I'd raise you off it
cleanse the little tear with a list, or erstwhile
fabricated substitute, like the sweet powdered
hard core from the blooming old shit store
I was wrong to say lie up there, but its ok
we're not gonna rule out a long term extension
as long as pure daylight stays out of the way

Deflategrets

we might as well start with the artificial hill on governor's
isle, or we might as well start with the way local street
violence deflates the pompous, the pretentious, the
grandiose dose of instant critical appraisal, no, we might
as well begin with the neglect of certain experiences
pumpkin carving say, due to tiny domestic compromises
anywhere's a place to be for the roach family, we might
as well count bag leafs, they're banned in Paris, I see
one know, shredded, I mean now, in a blank tree in
Sauer Park on 12th near B, where I write this amidst
people disguised as people, who don't kind of know me
maybe, the playground scene, a place where I'm getting
a degree in performing what realism looks like it means
to me, sitting quietly between negotiations, i.e., five year
old June just handed some gum to me, I chewed it &
handed it back and she fled with horrified glee, today
we both hate the letter e, the gum competes with a
browning yellow leaf for cheap mortality, & we might
as well start with an overpriced cup of lukewarm coffee
we might as well start with the addict on the C standing
nearby smelling like lower Manhattan in 1983, I fucked
up today (this tiny little dude just came by to say hi to me
anyway), not bringing the candy, & now J asks me to say
my name, but I make her do it: me & we no like that game

Pretergrets

plitch mleets flear flailure, brow lips delete man
prayer at stanza's stanzaic end, cover alms, amvette's
attired park, daddy why do you hate busytown saw
a pigeon wipe its ass with a twenty today, bad beak
showing up in vanishing point's bleak envy, a social
median's symptom of post-discerning availability, ear
is the ind iller, just saying forget truncated placating
up intricacy, distillation of likeness into one's endlessly
it's cool, I don't have to dig it, a creature on the side
dodging stories, gladiola wipeouts cloister on cloth
desire, approach sheaves but denuded in the casually
subterranean arena, everyone in Atlantis seems to be
blue, a blue you get when the painted brain gets velvety
crunch time touchable, slide to unlock your mystical
wistfulness, chuckled left in the guillaume light, national
splat month likes the poems with the orange powder
under their headbands, is your poise characteristical
boner compares cruise to lucifer, I thought charac-
teristical might rhyme with lucifer, but a heathenly
proforgot to demi-write lucefistical, want to say I better
end this shit soon, but no one's coming, Dagocles
liked to juggle haunting vicissitudes according to Dig-
dogenes, don't drop your micron when your umbil-
ical button's starts coming forward & taking names

Megrets

poet identifies with negative space hidden by
the index card, held together by dripping thread
& the allover action pigeons control, poet is not
assuming anyone knows what shame is, slapping
photographs of fossilized catastrophe, sun baked
onto stationways trains go by, poet's stain hums
its declining balance in an illusion of equilibrium
in New York poet can rent this podium for half a
grand per week, poet will leave the difficulty to
the panelees attendees & dig-resistant philosophies
poet don't dig doubt's unsalaried vibrations or
certainty's baffled strokes, it's all shit to spread on
the airways when the money gets waved, bacterial
ghostlings installing little doorlings, poet keeps
peeling dispersed compositions off poet's bodybrace
still likes being talked to by the air & talking back
walking against the psycho-electronic traffic, will
never stop swearing & swearing off, figures the music
makes it linear, senses the deliberate inability to not
quite remember's the skill of the ineffable fuckface
won't pat back at expense of pigeon siblings' backs

Gretgrets

bound loom mount hang, tapes obsidian, arranger
of corners cuddles space, pumice demands jersey 1
certain songs don't come on error on the dial in love
with "so I seem to be being instructed to peel off
off every layer of skin & gradually bleed out a map
of personal extinction," but I do this, hopping rides
on the backs of trash trucks, whole surfaces, paid to
self-invent, coming together to pull the present apart
I loathe metaphor, autumn rhythms loathe me back
shooting past into a fear only the insane don't take
for granted, stiff not stuff, arguably abstract, extended
villain, sham shame, zone fallen, pivot skin, held dark
dark care, books, rooms, I read too fucking fast, but
it works, push low power mode on to pull time into
sandwich mode, as we get older dad gets funnier, my
younger daughter possesses a version of his red-cheeked
humor, saying so makes me one of every sunuvabitch
who said he had rosy cheeks, his favorite band after
he died was the Jungle Brothers, I love to never go
on Sunday drives, even on weekdays, take that sane
storage, we shines hold that, the we, the blew and
brush, you know death is scared of notation, right?

Pregrets

couldn't tell difference between the craven & the
arisen, or was it the driven & the grave, the graven
the grover grave raisin ridden by warrior frogs into
the cloven fields of bacon, it, being that, & mystical
unlike and, the whole fat-free works, wasn't a diff-
erence I wanted the shell to tell, the whole fucking
stair was just levitating over my head, no amount
of arrogant self-deprecation gussied up as hand-
waving, away with yon dusky halo, is gonna bluff
that stair back into its on, but that's experience
for you, always twisting in the ball-do-lie too quickly
for visible turns, you do realize metaphor's a con-
version device, eating all the cheese puffs, their
brothers & their sisters, after ducking all the adult
brains afraid of poetry & its open claims on yr right
to unknown, man, one has a tremendous desire to
be slight, not slight like respecting the office slight
or kissing the ass in classical slight, or pretending
you've got the key to unlock the mobile from the
inside slight, ah three's enough for the number-fuckers
all that spit about unspended hearts, monstrous
dimension, like the pedestrian, you mean pederast
absence, god, you're so, "tonight I will do something
evil in this town," inadequate there Berrigan, is an
invention yr pulled away from, to let that it continue

Regrets

born implicated, a so-so-what in a run-down
enrichment program, logs rock photo lickers
& you won't forget to put gravy on our rose
a four-issue vendetta sings rounds, sleeper
devastated sheets with prevailing tincture
one of these directions says north to me
was sure I wasn't eternally alone on the roof
watching skywriting slice open the sky, don't
give in to the urge to cover every angle with
your mouth, mild audience, on the johnny
lam jones, looking with precarity at local
sleepers sold in window remnants, we can
do research to help them rethink the way
you move, scrutiny sucks, the little guy biscuit
pinky trod, Cold Blooded Old Times, Jams
Run Free, I regret the end of free-flowing
personal tension on a step-by-step slow refrain
basis, I regret sweet speed's ramp of deathyness
I regret taking every job, absorbing their muse-ish
explanatory alternatives scheming inside hives
of sanctity, I regret primary care, the key factor
disaligning in spaces to push the all-tone disguised
as vibe, elbows giving off slanky boomerang lines

Regrets

I regret knowing what time it's ever been, I regret
not painting Not The Bathroom on your white
walls in big indigo letters, I regret the feint
of leaning in in that death by snake landscape
that was collage, I regret all kinds of nothings
little beautiful timidities I don't long-view regret
it was a they, we added up, you have to give people
the space you didn't know how to take, you don't
you're a sorting mechanism, you're not actually
all slime, you're a very fierce frail piece of guy
supposedly you didn't turn around the last time
dad said goodbye, who needs to notice, you being
yourself don't quite work your shit out loud
enough for the novelistic everyfucks, sunny
helmet kiss on forearm, light repulsion, at deep
night I come all over the courtly pre-imagined
my interest in desperation lies only in that
sometimes I find myself having become
desperate, I know ghosts, they're being ordered
about, fucked as ever by limitation, a book
the size of your fingers told me to force it so
so I say a damned thing, with love crushed to
bring out flavor, your look at me way keeps feeling
space filled with massive nonparticipation, then
bodies force you to appear, to measure out the
exacting space to not die in, or be nondead already

Pregrets

shadows cut up into journal entries, defenestrated
refusals like a what, nothing, the other night's line
steps to me, they were all amused by their own
hatreds, selective outrages plied into acquired
mouths, shadows written as thieves, debunked
certainty what-nothings our flock-off, x amount
secs later the self-knocking door pitches its own
retinal shit fit to de-establish presence in exchange
for gravitas, there's a ton of dumbs in the on the spot
flaming edgeless arrow tracer digital in the flat and
the conversation raises its own rent, the all-white
painting reminds your you-substitute a budget's just
a snapshot for the support, not doing shit for years's
an illustration of scale, not ethics, marble over here
marble over there, later mr. bump said its hard to
paint nothing, I wrapped a glacial yak around my
space index & tried to sweat it off, that tree has
an ordinary mask in its bark, no it really does, I'm
really sitting in a marble terrace staring at a tree
with a mask-face on it, totally fucking with my gret
I started don't know when, now I'm here, here, here
here, here, here, here, here, here, here, here, here,
(do I leave the little spaces in between heres) will
this reproduce without margins & not be a photo
it's a totally misunderstood extension to put all them
heres in the wrong tense, ing in the gap notorious bed

Degrets

I'd like to dedicate the don't stop, and the entire
enormity of the past to negative space, out on a
cereal box resembling a quark, are you scared of
corners, and it's nonexistent if it is there, exchanging
one middle for another, and his feeling of space
flesh as his flesh, they as intel naturally ooze, observed
in the urbane of society sense with, & knowledgeable
of shrubs, orange netting appears to the mature
sinkhole's periphery as latent art history, flanked
by refuse in beards, there is a glad bag that never
self-dumps, cassettes ride cats into slumset, little fan
blade hugs star, orange & green pachyderm swills
recline on couch, to ambiguate a slanky grid, you
can't even get the little stuffed neon guy to flinch
dream only in on or off the given-from-a-mouth-
terms, I don't know how to talk about dealing
with space well, gnarled severed floating fingers
pick-digging the streets, you're tiredness is just
a little rebellion against your doubt, history looks
like a splendid hemorrhage trembling precisely
confronts itself in form of micro-Johnson, lime
wedge breath security, the little door floater
finding legs to linger with, all questions assumingly
brushed into purrview as erased marauders fan out
to address an invisible stamp on the unhinge

Regrets

I know the mountain pups, they won't believe
me, won't believe a roach can game the system
cloak & dagger caught in negative man's designer
drug shell, the hermit crab gently lay purse in
echo chamber, oh list, the momentum can't be-
come all over your living, oh feed, whine senses
its degradation & ducks out of the scrum, putting
on the thread of Ender Inciarte's roto auction
value, I hear Helmet coming on, ready to send
a bouquet to Nirvana from a driven nowhere, I
ran away from works but you won't believe it, my
truth tantrum may be verified by local help, I'm
cool with some yelling if so far is your admitted
destination, but I know you're higher than the
fantasy of enigma, you hairy paw of pink origin
handing me a steering wheel will only leave an
impression in reverse, let's go ruin their minds
by invitation I told my little blue box of dying
transitions, sorry if I'm interrupting your mock
snake, I'm willfully caught in a scrabbled fartrap
if the becomes the animals become symbols, we
imitate dissolution, the et als nod & win, Jim
stops tying my shoe & telling me I should know
how by now, can't delete the current continuities

Pregrets

signed sox into local millions, scooting over wet red
light, she fútbol beers me the deep mad face, she's
greater than 3, like, probably, you, inhaling predis-
position secretly messaged for dagliminal posterized
unsane pfffffttt, letters imitate icing, scripted donated
shuns, during all live love matches, I was always cool
with the floor, you could talk up being set off, green
eye surfaces set under couch shadow furry mutilation
quote book shoulders into sight, enter passcode fears
the garbage plate, the cash only bliminal proposal
the arena changes type color to reestablish its ment
it's so hard for dudes to have slightly less than total
blanklessly, calgary taking on the flames, analyst uni-
brow overwhelms the floating vision, game recap
caps itself from patrol car, zounds of the spotted
fed closet after closet of, I know why my hands are
widthdrawn, liek a sub-shake, & gets to call it, account
of coughling, & the well lit rainy dash, bing where
my so-called acktoolity I cares to layer, small bag of
integrity phases, small ack of micro-digression
smack refrain, small boog from which dead faces
alight to relieve, if you tweet at me a stage says
I'll put you in the bugs, with a pledge of temporary
solemnity we & you can suck cess fully duck expect
(sorry, ducks) which, tics aside, are guous to us

Pregrets

I spent a certain amount of cash at Forbidden Planet
Tower Records, the corner store on 9th & 1st, southeast
corner, the corner store on 9th & 1st southwest corner the
corner store on 7th & 1st, northwest corner, the
candy shop on 1st between 7th & 8th with the Mr. Do
stand-up video game, the pizza parlor on St. Mark's &
A, southwest corner with Moon Patrol, the candy shoppe
on A between 8th & 9th w/ Double Dragon, the corner
store on St. Mark's & A, northwest corner that preceded
Nino's Pizzeria, Oscar's newsstand on St. Mark's and 1st
Garibaldi's groceries with the buggy booberry cereal on
9th and 1st, northwest corner, the Yankee Stadium right
field bleachers, Gem Spa's video game alcove on the St.
Mark's side, & I want, I want to be paid properly for my
childhood acting career, no powdered candy, no welcome
to golden folks as forks, roll-tap consolation, it's gonna
be really really hurt, your shot, beard at bad & gives
still can't mishandle the low strike, low helicopter
hover in the pen, aluminum dog uploads obey the love-
me-principles, kick to metaphorical id, tomorrow's
probable parables charting chromophobes, the promise
of another person walking by makes an empty street
so frightening in the sketch, chase on the walk-off de-
flection, the walk-off bobble, splinter of consciousness
in the old open bowl head, don't tell the aleatories
they're being aggressive, a cabbie ran that candy shop
on 11th & 1st when it was a candy shop & he wasn't
a cabbie, he told me, front to back, through his cab's slot

Pregrets

the page torn itself out, on a plain line, with a curve
like the earth, its destroyers too busy with reality's
accreting encapsulation to notice, aubade with inter-
changeable centers in fear of opposition, one-two has
having tremendous chaste desires to be slights, don't
insert yr image thing there in that likeness, dig dug
with reactionary vegetables, pensive music sidles up
to brackets, I've got your whole back but ya got no
neck, in my backpack requilibrium vs. prequilibrium
(ahem, says Chip, circling the act of sequence), pitch
the shit or don't, there are many formaldehydes of
anti-expression, every five minutes adding five years
scale peers into traffic, let us now misapprehend
nature's inhospitable quality (butterfly *attacks*), private
life goes on the wing, so, "this" is like "it" pointing
to itself, or handing it to you, because "it" is the enigma
right? I mean, "it" is "it," you can't do anything with
"it," but "this" gets "it" right, puts "it" in your hand
or in your voice, yeah, it not only gives you "it", but
it gives you somebody giving you "it", right, which is
like... it's up front, in a way, whereas "it," "it is raining,"
is mystical, you know, it sure is, but it's also reality
I mean, it's real reality, whereas, it's possible that
you can't ever really say "this" when you mean "it"

Pregrets

zebra green matches temperaments with the stuffed
locals, what does realism mean to taxidermied me, red
copter rises slicing a scraper into outer cubicle dreams
six types of gull admonish a ferry driver's entry with
stick-legged glares of disbelief, "so that I may learn if
he has some beautiful secrets in architecture," corm-
orants wish to find the beautiful forms of ancient
buildings, and out of the pictural repertory of the
grotesques he, semi-invited back by job 43 for frag-
ment time, the conjured cormorant pops its bill
out the water out the window, in response to raising
money, in the ordinary ability to insert violently
in this "machine" of his, the expected contradictory
emblem of emotion, i.e., you have tremendous
hatred in your hate, I mean hearse, no hea-hea-ha-
art, from planar chamber 3/grid fragment aleph-
banana-disappearing 66, zebra trophy tint shading
non-jaundice yellow, "why be afraid of hate/it is
only there," failing to move internally while faces
are frozen into mimical masks, pound radar arranges
feldspar purrs into blooming rhythm of the shook
loose, the fresh pictorial intervention, the dum-dum
mystery flavor, the escapist fig as fondled contour

Pregrets

& being of the era in a kind of reproduction
salad toss, the heavy back wheel pushing your
flaming nostril race into foregrounds decorating
corners, you gain entry to the understanding of
every discrete thing, plaintive mess of certainties
we don't know dick shit or jack about each other
I in fact am talking to myself in a living room
doused in hairway to steven, the vape trails of
hair chalk, telling the voices how much meaner
the country's become, how internalized that
meanness feels for all the recent depthless volume
that the on-your-own quality of it all remains
unacknowledged, it reminds nowness of when
we used to talk to the holes in our pants, strangers
so inscrutable had stopped preying on our enigmatic
desperation for contact (nowness lived in the 80s
too you know) hello flying kick feint coming
at us, on the way out from Julian's Billiard
Academy with Doug Oliver, corn-kind type cuts
up the crypt, the ennobled shards go ordinary
we work too hard making them not go together

Freegrets III

frameshield forward bloom of a cosmic stain, up on
the sun's old weird edge of expanse, to dispense with
the bad news incubus service, Whalen calligraphy
tipsy at the Capital with Harry Smith film stills at off-
centers for imploded suckers phasing out of practice
with attention, shapes dispersed from a composed owl
that ain't ever gonna think "I'm an owl", cross-checking
credibility's what nothing with flooding & frequent
lightning, original hatch buckles, portal to nebulae, im-
probably red lava beads playing at surfacing, burning
grazes onto the enigma plane, yellow looks out & up
to the edge of a triple interior, a center obliterating
perspective for reformation's feint, we rhyme a lot,
raises concerns, top down coloration shroom view
receding geography flake-stains the way of the pixel
back into the trail, that red sharpens the forward edge
to make kindred forms estranged enough to signal
themselves, 1984 seeds seeing's change, ghosts a speculate
raining so hard the drops bounce multiply into rooms
heat fuzz pushing out of reference to authority, so as
to desire being lost may require lost's permission, the
desire to be lost brought forward by finding myself lost
untraining to project or training forever, entraining to
anti-project & anti-reflect in the intense heat's opening
depth, reminded out at the frame's corner, in an
untitled cosmos series, edges taking full extent as bleed

for/after Vivian Springford

Acknowledgments & dedication

Various versions of some of these poems have appeared in the following places: *6x6*, *Ladowich*, *Volt*, *Theme Can*, *elderly*, *Critical Quarterly*, *Bodlahem*, *otter*, *Ampersand*, *Banqueted Editions*, *Bold Faced Lays*, *White Wall Review*, *Equalizer*, *LiveMag!*, *Posit*, *Poets.org*, *Poetry Project Newsletter*, *Potes.argh*, *feelings journal*, *Poetry at Sangam*, *Harper's*, *Columbia Poetry Review*, *New Yorker*, *Bettering American Poetry Volume 3*, *Literati Quarterly*, *ham sandwiches anon*, & *In the Minds of My Brother*. Thanks to the many editors who took such particular chances.

My grateful thanks as well to:

Edwin Torres for including several Pregrets in *The Body In Language: An Anthology* & for all the shared on-going-ness

Ugly Duckling Presse for making a broadside with "Pregrets (how much time wasted waiting to be loved . . .)"

Justin Reed, Jessica Baran, and Ted Mathys for making a broadside with "Degrets (image production sells us our meltdowns . . .)" for the 100 Boots Poetry Series at the Pulitzer Arts Foundation in St. Louis

Jonathan Allen for a video collaboration involving "Pregrets (zebra green matches temperaments . . .)"

Paul Maziar and Couch Press for publishing a version of section III as the chapbook *Degrets*, and to Tom Burckhardt for the amazing cover.

Vagabond Press and Pam Brown for publishing a version of the first section as a chapbook, also called *Pregrets*

the Lower Manhattan Cultural Council for providing studio space on Governor's Island in the fall of 2015 that helped me recover from losing a notebook with twenty written but untyped poems that would have been part of this work

to the Robert Rauschenberg Residency & Robert Rauschenberg Foundation for providing the time and space in 2014 that helped me get this whole thing into gear

& to John Yau, Jasper Johns, Shanna Compton, Douglas Kearney, Edgar Arceneaux, Taylor Davis, Anne Waldman, Cedar Sigo, Karen Weiser, David Berrigan, Edmund Berrigan, Alice Notley, and John Coletti for keying in.

Pregrets is dedicated to Rod Smith, and to the painters.

Index of first lines

About the author

Anselm Berrigan is a poet, teacher, and editor of offhand accumulations. He is the author of various books, chap-books, and other idiosyncratic publications, including *Something for Everybody*, *Zero Star Hotel*, *They Beat Me Over the Head with a Sack*, *Free Cell*, *Notes from Irrelevance*, *Skasers* (with John Coletti), and *Come In Alone*. He is surviving in New York City, and teaching where the work is available.

Houdini word smithy Anselm Berrigan writes elsewhere about poetry coming from a place *as if a filter between your consciousness and the world fluttering in.* This magic act, not facile, is unpredictable—the filter works lovingly overtime, hard at its alchemy, arrangement, intuitive flowing "moves" of brain flash, found attitude, multiple voiced increments. Sometimes I'm breathless inside a language barrage or barrel speedily turning not bound by any one thought. Other times I'm with abandon in the cognition quotidian soup. ("The abstract poet runs where in cognito again?") But consciousness is a vivid Zen equalizer—a syncretic piling on as words jump the gate, rhapsodize, list, lumber, scan this wild existence. So what IS the sense of *Pregrets*? "gret" comes from the "greter" meaning to weep, mourn, lament from the Frankish "gretan". Was it that moment before you weep ? or imagined later? Future pluperfect? Regrets suggest a past. Begrets suggest something between begetting and beginning, more complicated than "first thought, best thought" And we have also Deflategrets, Freegrets, Megrets, Gretgrets, and then Degrets de-constructs the lament perhaps. So *Pregrets* I figure gets at origins that already have some kind of affect/karma but don't have to add up. A huge relief. This work is all about duration and mind and space, and Time as spiral. Often like dream text with that crazy "other" fluttering in wild tandem. "The escapist fig as fondled contour." Amazing.

—**Anne Waldman**